You're Not Alone

Resources to Help You through the Grief Journey

Brook Noel and Pamela D. Blair, Ph.D.

Fran King B.A., B.Ed., C.B.E., C.G.T.
Educational Consultant
Grief Therapist
OACCPP #1587-1
905 666 2129
fran.king@rogers.com

A GRIEFSTEPS® GUIDE

www.griefsteps.com

adapted from *I Wasn't Ready to Say Goodbye*
by Brook Noel and Pamela D. Blair, Ph.D.

Contents

Important Notes

Online Support: References are periodically made to the Grief Steps® online support group. You can learn more about this group at www.griefsteps.com

Professional Help: If at any point you fear you may do harm to yourself or someone around you, seek professional help immediately or contact your local emergency response service.

Chapter One
Getting Started

"When you are up against a wall, be still and put down roots like a tree, until clarity comes from deeper sources to see over the wall."
- Dr. Carl Jung

Be still, put down roots...very good advice to the survivor of loss who often feels as though they are a tree, standing alone, blowing sideways in the heavy storm of grief.

Survivors can feel isolated and may experience a loss of identity. Some may experience not only the clearly defined stages written about in counselors' handbooks but also a lingering sadness. You may be aching for the deceased. You may choose to consult with a pastoral counselor or grief therapist, but there are other sources—poetry, music, volunteer work, support groups, group therapy, self-help books and a variety of useful professional therapies which can frequently provide solace in unexpected ways. This guide is offers you an introduction to the many resources available to you.

Please note that one therapy or self-help avenue may work better for you than another. We all have unique needs and what will work best for you depends on your background and your belief system. We know there is no quick fix or cure for the upset and shock caused to our body, mind and spirit. Some of the therapies we've mentioned can help. We wish we could do more. Sometimes the best we can do for each other is listen. In the case of self-help therapies, you also need to listen to yourself. Allow your intuition to guide you to what you need. If you have any questions, don't hesitate to ask a trained professional for an opinion.

Chapter Two
Frequently Asked Questions

In Chapter Three you will find a collection of resources to help you on your pathway of grief. Some of these are organizations that offer support groups that meet face-to-face. Others offer groups that meet on-line. Still other organizations offer newsletters, free brochures or magazines, and many offer a combination of these services.

Some of these resources are available only via the Internet. Those resources are marked Internet Resource in parenthesis.

Before we go into the resource reviews, let's look at some frequently asked questions about self-help and therapy.

Frequently asked questions about self-help and therapy

Q. I've heard a lot about self-help. What kind of self-help should I try?

Journaling and Letter Writing
One of the most powerful tools for recovery is to write down your real thoughts and feelings in a journal—no editing or judgment. Writing a letter to

the deceased can also be comforting. Some of your initial feelings will be quite strong or angry. Don't let these strong emotions deter your efforts. You need to get those feelings out. After a while, your writing will turn softer as the emotional charge lessens. You have a unique and meaningful story to tell—the story of the beginning, middle and ending of a relationship. Telling your story, writing it in a journal, creating poems, hearing the stories of others...these are valid ways that we heal. For this exercise to be effective, no one has to read what you wrote although you may want to read portions of your journal to your support group members. One woman I spoke with said, "What worked best for me was to keep a daily gratitude journal so I could see that my life was full of more than just grief and loss. It helped me feel more balance and gave me a perspective that was empowering."

Telling or writing your story is a way to come alive again. In her book, *The Fruitful Darkness*, Joan Halifax reflects on our collective as well as personal stories when she writes "stories are our protectors, like our immune system, defending against attacks of debilitating alienation...They are the connective tissue between culture and nature, self and other, life and death, that sew the worlds together, and in telling, the soul quickens and comes alive."

In his classic book, *Reaching Out*, Henri Nouwen writes that though our own story "can be hard to tell, full of disappointments and frustrations, deviations and stagnations...it is the only story we have and there will be no hope for the future when the past remains unconfessed, unreceived and misunderstood."

Don't put any expectations or limitations on your writing—simply write. If you find it hard to get started, set a timer for five minutes and write anything that comes to mind. Don't stop. The writing may not make sense or be coherent, but it will help you get used to placing words on paper. Don't worry about spelling, grammar or style—just get the words out. Try doing five minute writing exercises each morning when you awake or at night before going to bed.

For those of you who would appreciate guidance from the Bible in your journaling, there is a wonderful Internet site at GriefShare. The area is called *"On Your Own: Daily Help and Encouragement."* The area guides you to sections of the Bible that are relevant to the feelings, emotions and questions a person deals with during grief. The site offers 13 weeks of personal devotions. Each week contains five daily Bible studies and suggestions for further reading. Each day also has an "In Your Life" area, which asks you questions to help you identify where you are in your journey from mourning to joy. You can access this tool at www.griefrecovery.com.

Take the time to find a way to tell your story. Listen to your story. Listen to the stories of others.

Self-Help Books

Reading entire books will no doubt be very difficult in the beginning. However, there are some wonderful books on grieving that can be helpful. Do not plan to read an entire self-help book from cover to cover. Simply find what you need most in the index or table of contents and read a page or two at a time. In time, you will be able to read more. A list of books is provided in the resources section of this book.

Q. I know I need group support but what kind of group is best for me? How do I know which one is right?

A support or therapy group can be the ideal place for you to inexpensively explore your feelings. Your previous circle of mutual friends may no longer be available to you, and a support group will be valuable in helping you re-establish your place in the world. Let's explore the basic group types.

A professionally led support group is organized and facilitated by a psychotherapist, pastoral counselor, psychologist, social worker or other mental health professional. You should feel supported and nurtured without judgment in this type of group. A fee may be charged since it is run by professionals.

A peer led support group is just that—led by someone who has experienced the death of a loved one and has decided to help others. Usually, it is someone who is at least a year or two into the grieving process. There is normally no fee, or perhaps a donation will be requested of you.

A professionally led therapy group requires you to be in private counseling with the professional running the group and is an adjunct to your therapy work. You may also feel supported and nurtured in this group, but the therapist may challenge you on some of the beliefs you have that get in the way of your healing.

Many organizations form groups. Hospitals and religious organizations sometimes sponsor these groups. Therapists and social workers also form groups. Finding the right group for you will be easier if you pay attention to your intuition during and after the first meeting. At a time when we aren't sure of our ability to make decisions, trust your gut feelings to guide you. And don't give up; keep trying until you find the "right fit."

Try the following exercise. The first time you go to a support or therapy group, take a pencil and paper with you. Either during or immediately after your session, jot down words that describe how you are feeling. Pay close attention to your feelings. Now do this again the second time you go, and once more on the third. Are you still feeling the same as you did the first time and second time? If your experience is mostly positive, continue with the group. If you notice you have written mostly about anxiety, fear, stress or shame, then stop going. Keep looking until you find a group that gives you positive feelings. Remember, a group is meant to be part of your extended support system. Take into account however, that you will not feel uplifted each time you go because the grieving process takes time and is full of its own ups and downs, set backs and hurdles.

The stories of loss we have heard are as diverse as fingerprints—each one slightly different from the next. When we gather with those who attend and begin sharing, the connections, one to another, are astounding. Regardless of where we are in the process of grieving, or how we lost our loved one, we become supportive, relating and recognizing each other's pain almost immediately. This sense of community and acceptance is vitally important to our spiritual and emotional healing.

There are some questions you will want to ask the person who is in charge:

- Is there a fee?
- How often do you meet?
- Is there an attendance requirement?
- Is it mandatory to share or speak at the group?
- How many people are there in the group? (If the group is larger than 10, you may not get your needs met as readily. There is only so much time for each person.)
- Is the group for men/women only? A group consisting of women only will help women develop supportive female relationships; and,

likewise, a group of all men will help men safely express their feelings.

Allow the group the opportunity to "give" to you. Let them know if you have a need to be hugged or held–and be clear if touching you or holding you is uncomfortable for you. Work on believing you have earned the right to receive. Don't be afraid to talk about or express your feelings. After all, that's why you came. You will not receive the support you came for if you hold back. Think about friends in your life and realize that it was with time that the level and depth of their friendship was revealed—the same is true in a group experience.

Q. Maybe I'm spending too much time alone. Is this bad for me?

Solitude is as important as a group experience. In solitude comes the opportunity (if we are not afraid) to slow down, to reflect, to gain a deeper inner vision of our responsibilities, our needs and ourselves. However, if we spend too much time alone, we risk believing the inner voices that can overwhelm us, so you may do better if you attend a weekly support group in conjunction with your alone time. A group offers the opportunity to check out what we "learned" in solitude and to find out if what we've been telling ourselves is helpful and true.

Q. Everyone is saying I should find group support, but I can't seem to find anything in my area.

Try looking in the yellow pages or online. Some of the ways these groups are listed or advertised are:

- Bereavement group
- Bereavement support
- Newly widowed
- Young and widowed
- Parents of murdered children
- Suicide support

If you can't find a group in your area, you may want to start one. Talk to your local library. Many libraries have a community room they will let you use for no charge. Talk to a minister, priest or rabbi in your community—find out if they would be willing to organize a group and have you be the contact person. You don't have to go the course of loss alone! Many existing groups offer starter materials for forming a group. Contact national headquarters in the resources section for these offerings. Also keep in mind that the Internet has opened up worlds of support. The great thing about the Internet is that you can "sign on" whenever you need support. See the Internet Resources for ideas.

Q. I'm a man and it seems like all this self-help and group support stuff is for women. I'm afraid I won't find the help I need.

Men grieve differently from women. They are often silent, solitary mourners who immerse themselves in activities and private, symbolic rituals. They have a tendency to approach grief in a cognitive way and may be judged as cold and uncaring. Men feel profoundly, but often cannot express the depth of their loss—even to intimates.

Men have a tendency to "tough it out" rather than seek support. But when they do find support, they most often find a strong bond with the other men and a safe place to express feelings. Ken expressed great relief when he spoke with tears in his eyes, "And I thought I was the only guy in New York whose heart was being ripped out every time I looked at my wife and saw my daughter in her face." There is no "manly" way to grieve, the experts say. There are many ways to cope with loss that have more to do with personality than gender. However, there is a stereotype for a man who loses his wife for instance—two or three months of sadness, then "suck it up" and get on with living.

There are eight widows for every widower among the 13 million widowed people in the United States. Little wonder men who lose their wives feel adrift. Society expects men to "walk tall" through their grief, yet offers little male-related support.

Jim Conway, a minister and author of *Men in Mid-Life Crisis,* believes in group therapy. Jim joined four grief groups after the death of his wife. Conway likens grief groups to Alcoholics Anonymous. "You don't have to explain what it means when you say, 'I am grieving.' I need to go and sit and listen and cry. I needed to know I'm normal. By the time a year was over, I knew I needed to move on when my primary purpose turned from being helped to helping others."

The Internet can come in handy here as well. We found several pages for grief sponsored by men. Read through the Internet Resources section of the last chapter for ideas. You may also want to review our section on "Men and Grief in the Losing a Child" chapter.

Q. I'm considering attending a support group once a week. Will going to a group help me cope even when I can't attend?

When you commit to a bereavement support or therapy group, you "take the members with you" when you go into difficult situations. You are never really alone. Sometimes if you ask, members will go with you not just in spirit, but also in the flesh. For example, Maureen had to go to the city hall to pick up her son's death certificate, and she expressed her anxiety and fear to the group. After she admitted she was scared that she might break down in a public place, Shelly, another group member, volunteered to accompany and drive her if she wanted.

Q. My friends and family all say I need the support of others who have gone through this, but I don't feel ready to talk about this face-to-face. Are there any alternatives?

Fortunately, there are. The Internet has opened up many avenues to exchange and share information. One of the most popular features of the Internet is chat rooms. While many chat rooms have no designated topic or are not moderated, there are many that offer grief support, specifically. The Internet Resources section found in Chapter Nineteen and the Appendix list several such groups. You can listen or read other's stories and share as you choose. You can also remain anonymous. Another advantage is that you can seek help when you need it. If you are feeling low in the middle of the night, you can simply "sign on" to your computer and find someone to comfort you.

Chapter Three
Supportive Publications

Bereavement Publishing
Bereavement Publishing cares for the bereaved by providing resources. *Bereavement Magazine* functions as a "support group in print." They also offer a "Grief in the Workplace" program to help Corporate America understand the needs of grieving employees. The group offers a magazine, 15 booklets, books, gift baskets and products, teaching tapes and a catalog. For more information contact: Bereavement Publishing, Inc., 4765 North Carefree Circle, Colorado Springs, CO 80917-2118 or call (888) 604-HOPE (4673). Access the website at: www.bereavementmag.com.

Concern for Dying
After experiencing a sudden loss, it is common for people to want to get their own affairs in order. The Concern for Dying organization provides resources that can help. *The Living Will* and *Durable Power of Attorney* are two documents that they will supply free upon request. Contact information: 250 West 57th Street, New York, NY 10107 or by calling (212) 246-6962.

One Caring Place
One Caring Place publishes many pamphlets dealing with difficult emotions like grief, anger and loss.

Brief and to the point, these caring publications offer wonderful support. You can contact them for a complete list of their publications by calling toll-free (800) 325-2511 or by writing to One Caring Place, Abbey Press, St. Meinrad, IN 47577. The website can be viewed at www.carenotes.com.

The Centering Corporation
The Centering Corporation supports grieving people and those who care for and love them. They provide supportive resources for families, individuals, professional caregivers and friends. The organization was founded in 1978 and offers a free Creative Care Package Catalog. The catalog features over 200 books to support those experiencing grief or loss. You can request the catalog by calling (402) 553-1200 or by writing to: The Centering Corporation, 7230 Maple Street, Omaha, NE 68134.

Chapter Four
Support for Loss of a Partner

American Association
of Retired Persons – Widowed Persons Service
"The AARP Widowed Persons Service (WPS) is a community-based program in which trained, widowed volunteers reach out to the newly widowed. Established in 1973 and based on the 'Widow to Widow' research of Dr. Phyllis Silverman, WPS is a self-help program offering one-to-one support, group work, public education, a telephone and referral service, and an outlet for rebuilding life as a single person. To locate the closest AARP Widowed Persons Service program in your community, call (888) 687-2277. Additionally, AARP offers many helpful brochures including, *On Being Alone—A Guide for Widowed Persons; Final Details; Reflections and Suggestions on Making New Friends;* and *When an Employee Loses a Loved One.* Their web site also contains comprehensive information, links and resources for dealing with grief. You can visit their web site at http://www.aarp.org. They also hold online grief support chats three days per week on America Online. Visit their website for further details. You can write to them at 601 E. Street NW, Washington, DC 20049.

Death & Dying (Internet Resource)
This site offers comprehensive support for widows and widowers. They have a monthly newsletter that is delivered via e-mail and a moderated chat room. They also have message boards. Check out their offerings at http://www.beyondindigo.com/.

National Association of Military Widows
This group provides referral services for the newly widowed, sponsors social events and support groups, and lobbies for legislation beneficial to military widows. Contact them at 4023 25th Road North, Arlington, VA 22207 or call (703) 527-4565.

Society of Military Widows (SMW)
This group serves the interests of women whose husbands died on active duty military service or during retirement from the armed forces. They can be contacted by calling (800) 842-3451 or e-mailing at webmaster@militarywidows.org. Write to: 5535 Hempstead Way, Springfield, VA 22151. Visit the website at http://www.militarywidows.org/.

THEOS
(They Help Each Other Spiritually) International
THEOS International has groups in both the United States and Canada that support widows and widowers. They also publish a magazine, book and organizational materials. For more information write: THEOS, 322 Boulevard of the Allies, Suite 105, Pittsburgh, PA 15222-1919. THEOS can be contacted by phone at (412) 471-7779.

Beginning Experience
This organization offers international support programs for divorced, widowed and separated adults and their children, enabling them to work through the grief of a lost marriage. They can be contacted at: 1657 Commerce Drive, South Bend, IN 46628 or call (574) 283-0279 or toll-free in US and Canada (866) 610-8877. The website can be found at: http://www.beginningexperience.org/.

To Live Again
This mutual help organization is for widowed men and women who support one another through the grief cycle. Contact them at P.O. Box 415, Springfield, PA 15222 or call (610) 353-7740.

WidowNet (Internet Resource)
This is the most comprehensive site we've found for those who are widowed. WidowNet is an information and self-help resource created for, and by, widows and widowers. "Topics covered include grief, bereavement, recovery, and other information helpful to people, of all ages, religious backgrounds and sexual orientations, who have suffered the death of a spouse or life partner." You can access the site at http://www.fortnet.org/WidowNet/. They also have an IRC Chat. The group is most active on Tuesdays, Thursdays and Fridays after 8:00pm.

Books about the loss of a partner

How to Go On Living When Someone You Love Dies by Therese A. Rando, Ph.D., New York, Bantam, 1991—Includes suggestions for ways to deal with sudden or anticipated death. Offers self-help techniques to work on unfinished business, take care of the self and when to get help from others. Leads you through the painful but necessary process of grieving and helps you find the best way for yourself. Offers guidance to help you move into your new life without forgetting your treasured past.

Grief Expressed: When a Mate Dies by Marta Felber. Fairview Press, 2002—This compassionate workbook guides you through the process of grieving the death of a mate. Sensitive writing and practical exercises help you to address issues such as loneliness, building a support system, managing sleepless nights, finances, self-nurturing and much more. The author has drawn from her counseling background, as well as her own self-healing after the death of her husband.

Widow to Widow: Thoughtful Practical Ideas for Rebuilding you Life by Genevieve Davis Ginsburg, M.S., Perseus Publishing, 1997—The author writes from her own experience as a widow and therapist. The book is frankly honest and attempts to dispel myths, disputes the rules and encourages the widow to begin her new life in her own way and time.

When Your Spouse Dies: A Concise and practical source of help and advice by Cathleen L. Curry, Ave Maria Press, 1990—This short book deals with a variety of practical topics within a spiritual framework. Included are topics such as advice on loneliness and sexuality, financial priorities and planning, and good health practices.

Living with Loss: Meditations for Grieving Widows by Ellen Sue Stern, Doubleday, 1995—This book, small enough to fit in a purse, is full of supportive and empowering reflections. This daily companion is designed to help you cope today, cherish yesterday and thrive tomorrow.

Chapter Five
Support for Grieving Children

Camp "Good Grief"

Camp "Good Grief" is a summer camp program which offers grief education workshops and provides support and understanding for youth ages 12-16, who have experienced the death of a sibling, parent, grandparent or close friend. The camp is held in New York. For more information visit the web site at http://www.baptistonline.org/services/community/ca mps/good_grief.asp#ggrief or call (901) 227-7121 or toll-free (800) 895-4483.

KIDSAID (Internet Resource)

KIDSAID is an extension of GriefNet, which is a comprehensive Internet community that has provided support to over 3 million people in the last year. The KIDSAID area provides a safe environment for kids and their parents to find information and ask questions. To learn more about KIDSAID, visit http://kidsaid.com/.

Motherless Daughters, Inc.

This national organization was founded in 1995 and now has 46 affiliated groups. They provide support, community and resources to women and girls who have experienced early mother loss. Information and referals, national conferences, a newsletter, phone support and pen pals are available. Contact Motherless Daughters, Inc by calling (212) 614-8047 or visit them online for further information at http://motherlessdaug.meetup.com/.

RAINBOWS

RAINBOWS provides curriculum and training for establishing peer support groups for children, adolescents and adults who are grieving a death, divorce or other painful transition in their family. Contact this group at: http://www.rainbows.org/, e-mail info@rainbows.org, write to RAINBOWS Headquarters, 2100 Golf Road #370, Rolling Meadows, IL 60008, or call toll-free (800) 266-3206.

The Dougy Center for Grieving Children

This group, founded in 1982, offers two outlets—one for the region of Portland, Oregon and another that is national in scope. Through the National Center for Grieving Children & Families, this group offers support and training locally, nationally and internationally to individuals and organizations seeking to assist children and teens in grief. The mission of the Dougy Center for Grieving Children is to provide to families in Portland and the surrounding regions, loving support in a safe place where children, teens and their families, grieving a death, can share their experiences as they move through their healing process. You can learn more about these programs by contacting The Dougy Center at (503) 775-5683, emailing help@dougy.org or visiting the website at http://www.dougy.org/. You can also write The Dougy Center at: P.O. Box 86852, Portland, OR 97286.

Books for children, teens and their caregivers

A Taste of Blackberries by Doris B. Smith, HarperTrophy, 1992 (8-9 years)—The author conveys the experience and feelings of an eight-year-old boy whose best friend Jamie dies unexpectedly. The boy and his family, along with Jamie's family, deal with the myriad of questions and feelings engendered by this unexpected event.

Breaking the Silence: A Guide to Help Children with Complicated Grief by Linda Goldman, Western Psychological Services, Los Angeles, CA, Routledge, 2001—Designed for both mental health professionals and parents, this book provides specific ideas and techniques to use in working with children who have suffered psychological trauma from violence, homicide, suicide or other traumas. Explains how to break the silence and then how to help children recover.

Coping with Death and Grief by Marge Eaton Heegaard, Lerner Publications, 1990—Includes stories about young people, grades 3-6, who deal with grief. Provides facts about death that are developmentally based.

Don't Despair on Thursdays! (ages 4-12) by Adolph Moser, Ed.D., Western Psychological Services, Los Angeles, CA, Landmark Editions, Inc, 1996—This gentle book lets children know that it's normal to grieve in response to loss and that grief may last more than a few days or weeks. Offers practical suggestions that children can use, day by day, to cope with the emotional pain they feel. Young readers will be comforted by the reassuring text and colorful illustrations.

Goodbye Rune (ages 5-11), by Marit Kaldhol and Wenche Oyen, Western Psychological Services, Los Angeles, CA, Kane/Miller Book Publishers, 1991— Rune and Sara are best friends, until the day that Rune accidentally drowns. This is a sensitive account of a child's first experience with death. Sara asks her parents endless questions, and their patient answers help her come to terms with the loss of someone special. She comes to realize that, through her memories, Rune will always be with her. Explores death and grief in terms children can understand.

Helping Bereaved Children, edited by Nancy Boyd Webb, DSW, Western Psychological Services, Guilford Publications, Inc., 2002—This book for therapists includes therapeutic interventions for children who have suffered a loss. Individual chapters focus on such topics as, death of a grandparent, father or mother, accidental sibling death, suicide of mother, violent death of both parents, traumatic death of a friend, sudden death of a teacher and more.

Part of Me Died, Too: Stories of Creative Survival among Bereaved Children and Teenagers by Virginia Lynn Fry, 1995, Dutton Children's Books, NY— Eleven true stories about young people who experienced the loss of family members or friends in a variety of ways including, murder, suicide and accident. Includes writings, drawings, farewell projects, rituals and other creative activities to help children bring their feelings out into the open.

Talking About Death: A Dialogue between Parent and Child by Earl A. Grollman, Beacon Press, 1991—How do you explain the loss of a loved one to a child? This compassionate guide for adults and children to read together features an illustrated read-along story, answers to questions children ask about death, and comprehensive lists of resources and organizations that can help. Helpful for children from preschool to preteen.

The Good Mourning Game by Nicholas J. Bisenius, Ph.D. and Michele Norris, MSW, Western Psychological Services, Los Angeles, CA—Using an artistically designed game board, this resource is a wonderful therapy tool for children who've suffered a loss. The board illustrates nature's basic cycle, which, like the grief cycle, moves from stormy intensity to relative calm. It can be played by a therapist and one to three children in usually about 45 minutes.

The Grieving Child: A Parents Guide by Helen Fitzgerald. Simon & Schuster Adult Publishing Group, 1992—Compassionate advice for helping a child cope with the death of a loved one. Also addresses visiting the seriously ill, using age-appropriate language, funerals, and more.

What on Earth do You do When Someone Dies? (ages 5-10) by Trevor Romain, Western Psychological Services, Los Angeles, CA, Free Spirit Publishing, Inc., 1999—Someone you love dies, and your whole world changes. Written to and for kids, this little book offers comfort and reassurance to children who've lost a loved one. It answers questions children often ask such as, Why? What next? Is it my fault? What's a funeral? Is it still okay to have fun? Will I ever feel better? Includes a list of practical coping strategies.

When Something Terrible Happens: Children can Learn to Cope with Grief, Library Binding, 1992 (ages 6-12) and *When Someone Very Special Dies: Children can learn to cope with grief*, Woodland Press, 1992 by Marge Eaton Heegaard,—These two books teach basic concepts of death and help children, through their workbook format, to express feelings and increase coping skills. Children use their own personal stories to complete the pages as they draw events and their accompanying feelings.

Chapter Six
Support for the Loss of a Child

**Aiding a Mother and Father
Experiencing Neonatal Death (AMEND)**
This organization strives to offer support and encouragement to parents grieving the loss of an infant through miscarriage, stillbirth or neonatal death. To learn more, write to 4324 Berrywick Terrace, St. Louis, MO 63128 or call (314) 291-0892.

Alive Alone
Alive Alone is an organization for the education and charitable purposes to benefit bereaved parents, whose only child or all children are deceased, by providing a self-help network and publications to promote communication and healing, to assist in resolving their grief, and a means to reinvest their lives for a positive future. The group offers a newsletter subscription and special events. Contact information: email alivalon@bright.net or write to 11115 Dull Robinson Road, Van Wert, OH 45891. The website is http://www.alivealone.org/.

Bereaved Parents of the USA
This national organization was founded in 1995 to aid and support bereaved parents and their families who are struggling to survive their grief after the death of a child. Information and referrals, a newsletter, phone support, conferences and meetings are available.

They also offer assistance in starting a support group. You may contact them at P.O. Box 95, Park Forest, IL 60466 or by calling (708) 748-7866. Visit the website: http://www.bereavedparentsusa.org/.

Center for Loss in Multiple Birth (CLIMB)
This International network was founded in 1987 to support parents who have experienced the death of one or more of their twins or higher multiples during pregnancy, birth, infancy or childhood. They offer a newsletter, information on specialized topics, pen pals, phone support, materials for twin clubs and loss support groups. Contact them by phone at (907) 222-5321 or by writing to P.O. Box 91377, Anchorage, AK 99509. Access the website at http://www.climb-support.org/.

Committee to Halt Useless
College Killings (CHUCK)
This national network was founded in 1979 to support families who have lost a child to hazing or alcohol in fraternity, sorority or other college groups. They educate on the dangers of these practices and offer information, referrals and phone support. Contact CHUCK at P.O. Box 188, Sayville, NY 11782 or call (516) 567-1130.

Hannah's Prayer
This International support group was formed to help those facing infertility, stillbirth and infant loss. They hold a Christian focus. You can contact them at: P.O. Box 168, Hanford, CA 93232-0168, e-mail Hannahs@Hannah.org, call or fax (281) 485-8986, or visit the website at www.hannah.org/.

Mothers in Sympathy and Support (MISS)

"The mission of Mothers in Sympathy & Support is to allow a safe haven for parents to share their grief after the death of a child. It is our hope that within these pages you discover courage, faith, friendship and love: The *courage* to speak out about your child and the love you have, regardless of the age or cause of death; The *faith* and reassurance that one day, we will all be reunited with our children—this time for eternity; *friendships* with other families experiencing this tragedy; and finally, it is our hope that you discover the enormity and depth of the *love* you have for your child. A love that transcends time and distance; heaven and earth; life and death. MISS provides support to parents enduring the tragedy of stillbirth, neonatal death and infant death from any cause including SIDS, congenital anomalies, trisomy 13. Grief education for parents and professionals is our main focus. We must realize that the grief journey lasts a lifetime. Our child has changed our lives forever. Come with us and get lost in our pages...find healing, honesty, hope and a rediscovery of yourself." Visit this valuable web site on the Internet at http://www.misschildren.org/.

Mommies Enduring Neonatal Death (MEND)

MEND is a nonprofit corporation whose purpose is to reach out to those who have lost a child due to miscarriage, stillbirth or early infant death and offer a way to share experiences and information through meetings, a bi-monthly newsletter and Internet web site. You may contact them at P.O. Box 1007,

Coppell, TX 75019 or call (888) 695-MEND, visit the website at http://www.mend.org or e-mail rebekah@mend.org.

Mothers Against Drunk Driving

Mothers Against Drunk Driving is a non-profit grass roots organization with more than 600 chapters nationwide. "MADD is not a crusade against alcohol consumption. Our focus is to look for effective solutions to the drunk driving and underage drinking problems, while supporting those who have already experienced the pain of these senseless crimes." MADD offers support groups and resources. You can search for a chapter near you on their web site at http://www.madd.org or by e-mail at Info@madd.org or contact their national office at 511 E. John Carpenter Freeway; Suite 700, Irving, TX 75062. Call (800) GET-MADD (438-6233).

National SIDS Resource Center

The National Sudden Infant Death Syndrome Resource Center (NSRC) provides information services and technical assistance on sudden infant death syndrome (SIDS) and related topics. Their goal is to promote an understanding of SIDS and provide comfort to those affected by SIDS through information sharing. NSRC's products and services include information sheets and other publications such as *What is SIDS, Sudden Infant Death Syndrome: Some Facts You Should Know,* and *Facts About Apnea and Other Apparent Life-Threatening Events*; Annotated bibliographies on SIDS and related topics from NSRC's databases, such as *Infant Positioning and Sudden Infant Death Syndrome,*

Smoking and Sudden Infant Death Syndrome, Children's Grief, and *SIDS and Epidemiology;* Reference and referral services related to SIDS research, bereavement and public awareness about SIDS. To contact NSRC call, write, or e-mail: National Sudden Infant Death Syndrome Resource Center, 2070 Chain Bridge Road, Suite 450, Vienna, VA 22182, toll free phone: (866) 866-7437, e-mail: sids@circlesolutions.com or visit the website at http://www.sidscenter.org/.

Parents of Murdered Children, Inc. (POMC)
Charlotte and Bob Hullinger in Cincinnati, Ohio founded POMC in 1978, after the murder of their daughter. What began as a small group, is now a national organization with over 300 chapters and contact people throughout the United States and abroad. The group provides the "ongoing emotional support needed to help parents and other survivors facilitate the reconstruction of a 'new life' and to promote a healthy resolution. Not only does POMC help survivors deal with their acute grief, but with the criminal justice system as well." The staff of the national headquarters of POMC will assist you, and if possible link you to others in your vicinity who have survived a loved one's homicide. In addition the staff can provide individual assistance and support. Should there be no chapter of POMC near you, they can aid you in starting one, if you wish. POMC also trains professionals in the fields of law enforcement, mental health, social work, community services, law, criminal justice, medicine, education and other fields that wish to learn more about survivors of homicide and the aftermath of murder. You may contact the

National Headquarters at 100 East Eighth Street, Suite B-41, Cincinnati, OH 45202 or call toll-free: (888) 818-POMC or visit their website at: www.pomc.com.

.

PenParents
Pen-Parents officially began its journey in April of 1988 in San Diego, California. Founder Maribeth Wilder Doerr, a bereaved parent, envisioned the need for a "pen-pal" network to help those who didn't feel comfortable with support group meetings or for those who lived in areas where traditional groups weren't available. The small kitchen-table operation has grown to over 800 members. This group serves as a support network of grieving parents who have experienced pregnancy loss or the death of a child(ren) through adulthood. They provide an opportunity for bereaved parents to talk about their child(ren) through a pen-pal type service by networking them with others in similar situations. You may visit their website at http://www.penparents.org or e-mail for information at penparents@penparents.org.

Pregnancy and Infant Loss Center
The Pregnancy and Infant Loss Center offers referrals for bereaved families experiencing miscarriage, stillbirth and infant death. Contact them at: 1421 E. Wayzata Blvd., #70, Wayzata, MN 55391 or call (612) 473-9372.

Save Our Sons and Daughters (SOSAD)
SOSAD offers crisis intervention and a violence prevention program that provides support and

advocacy for survivors of homicide or other traumatic loss. They offer weekly bereavement groups, professional grief counseling and training, education on peace movement to youth, advocacy, public education, a monthly newsletter, conferences, rallies and assistance in starting support groups. Contact SOSAD at 2441 W. Grand Blvd, Detroit, MI 48208 or call (313) 361-5200.

SHARE: Pregnancy & Infant Loss Support, Inc.
This group offers support to those who have lost a child during pregnancy or infancy. Their extensive web site offers a chat room and many valuable reading areas. Additionally they offer a free newsletter. You can visit their web site at www.nationalshareoffice.com/ or you may contact them at: National SHARE Office, St. Joseph Health Center, 300 First Capitol Drive, St. Charles, Missouri 63301-2893, Phone: (800) 821-6819. Send e-mails to share@nationalshareoffice.com. All of SHARE's information packets, correspondence and support are free of charge for bereaved parents. They also publish a bi-monthly newsletter that is available to bereaved parents, free of charge for the first year.

SIDS Network: A World of Information and Support (Internet Resource)
This web site details Sudden Infant Death and Other Infant Death. Go to http://sids-network.org/ for an incredibly comprehensive and valuable web site. At last look, the site contained over 1000 files with information on, or related to SIDS. This is a very well done site for anyone seeking support or information about SIDS.

SIDS Alliance
The SIDS Alliance was established in 1987 in an effort to unite parents and friends of SIDS victims with medical, business and civic groups concerned about the health of America's babies. You can locate an alliance near you by visiting their web site at http://www.sidsalliance.org or by calling (800) 221-7437, available 24 hours a day. Send e-mail to info@sidsalliance.org. Write to: Sudden Infant Death Syndrome Alliance, 1314 Bedford Avenue, Suite 210, Baltimore, MD 21208.

The Canadian Foundation for the Study of Infant Deaths - The SIDS Foundation
The Canadian Foundation for the Study of Infant Deaths is a federally registered charitable organization, which was incorporated in 1973 to respond to the needs of families experiencing a sudden and unexpected infant death. They offer some valuable brochures including: *Information about Sudden Infant Death Syndrome, When Your Baby has Died of Sudden Infant Death Syndrome, Having Another Child After a SIDS Death, Facts You Should Know About SIDS* and others. You may contact the resource by writing to: Suite 308, 586 Eglinton Avenue East, Toronto, ON, Canada M4P 1P2 or by calling (416) 488-3260 or by faxing (416) 488-3864 or visit http://www.sidscanada.org.

The Compassionate Friends
The mission of The Compassionate Friends is to assist families in the positive resolution of grief following the death of a child and to provide information to help others be supportive. There are

575 Compassionate Friends chapters. You can locate the one nearest you online at http://www.compassionatefriends.org/states.shtml. For a chapter's contact number and meeting information, call the National Office at (630) 990-0010. TCF also offers many helpful brochures. The brochures cover many areas such as: *Understanding Grief When a Child Dies, Understanding Grief When a Grandchild Dies, The Grief of Stepparents When A Child Dies, When a Brother or Sister Dies, Caring for Surviving Children, How Can I Help When A Child Dies?, The Death of An Adult Child* and many others. TCF also publishes a magazine for $20 per year. You can subscribe to the quarterly magazine by contacting the national office. Write: The Compassionate Friends, Inc., P.O. Box 3696, Oak Brook, IL 60522 or e-mail for more information: nationaloffice@compassionatefriends.org.

Trip's Heavenly Angels (Internet Resource)
Trip's Heavenly Angels is for parents who have lost a child or children through illness, accidents, miscarriage or stillbirth. An active and comforting online forum, including chat rooms, message boards, inspirational writings, gatherings and more. Website: www.groww.com/Branches/heavenly.htm.

Unite, Inc.
This national organization, founded in 1975, has 14 groups. They offer support for parents grieving miscarriage, stillbirth and infant death. They have group meetings, phone help, a newsletter and an annual conference. For more information contact UNITE, c/o Jeanes Hospital, 7600 Central Avenue,

Philadelphia, PA 19111 or call (215) 728-4286. Visit the website at http://www.unite.freeservers.com/ or e-mail UNITEINC1975@aol.com.

Books about the loss of a child

A Broken Heart Still Beats: After Your Child Dies edited by Anne McCracken and Mary Semel, Hazelden, 2000—Edited by two mothers who have lost a child, this book combines articles and excerpts—some fiction, some nonfiction—that featured the death of a child. A brief introduction to each chapter, describes a different stage of the grieving process and how it affected their lives.

After the Darkest Hour the Sun Will Shine Again : A Parent's Guide to Coping With the Loss of a Child by Elizabeth Mehren, Simon & Schuster Adult Publishing Group, 1997—This inspiring guide to coping with the loss of a child combines the author's own story with the experiences and wisdom of others who have gone through this tragedy.

The Worst Loss: How Families Heal from the Death of a Child by Barbara D. Rosof, Henry Holt & Co., Inc., 1995—The death of a child overwhelms many people. This book describes the losses that the death of a child brings to parents and siblings as well as potential PTSD reactions and work of grief. A very thorough and wise book. One of our favorite books on the topic.

When Goodbye Is Forever : Learning to Live Again After the Loss of a Child by John Bramblett , Random House, 1991—In 1985, John and Mairi Bramblett's youngest child, two-year-old Christopher, died in an accident, leaving them and their three older children devastated by shock and grief. Four months later, John began writing this deeply moving and honest story of how he and his family coped with the nearly unbearable pain of losing their son. *When Goodbye is Forever* walks us along the author's path to acceptance and recovery, taking us through the first hours and days of the tragedy, the painful but necessary first outings, and such occasions as Christopher's birthday, and the anniversary of his death. Mairi and the children share their responses to the tragedy as well, showing us the effect such a tragedy can have on the whole family.

Chapter Seven
General Bereavement Support

ACCESS:

Air Craft Casualty Emotional Support Services

ACCESS provides comfort to friends and families of air disaster victims and survivors. ACCESS helps people cope with their grief and pain by connecting them to grief mentors who have also survived or lost loved ones in an air tragedy. ACCESS is there for as long as the grieving need support. They can be contacted at 1594 York Avenue, Suite 22, New York, NY 10028, (877) 227-6435. Visit their website at www.accesshelp.org or e-mail info@accesshelp.org.

Bereavement and Hospice Support Netline

This is a national online public service directory of bereavement support groups and hospice bereavement services. It's sponsored by the Hospice Foundation of America and the University of Baltimore. For information, write to the University of Baltimore, SPANision of Applied Psychology and Quantitative Methods, 1420 North Charles Street, Baltimore, MD 21201. Call (410) 837-5310 or e-mail wclewell@UBmail.ubalt.edu.

Concerns of Police Survivors, Inc. (COPS)
This national association provides services to surviving friends and families of law enforcement officers killed in the line of duty. COPS can be contacted at PO Box 3199, 3096 S. State Highway 5, Camdenton, Missouri 65020; by calling (573) 346-4911 or by e-mail at cops@nationalcops.org. Visit COPS at www.nationalcops.org.

GriefNet (Internet Resource)
GriefNet is an Internet community consisting of more than 30 e-mail support groups and two web sites. Over three million people have visited the website in the last year. A very supportive site. Visit it at http://rivendell.org/.

GriefShare (Internet Resource)
This internet resource provides a comprehensive support group directory, special resources and a bookstore. Additionally, they have a wonderful area about journaling and a thirteen-week-guide with a Christian focus that includes scriptures, ideas for writing and journal pages you can print. Visit their site at http://www.griefrecovery.com/.

GROWW (Internet Resource)
GROWW is an independent haven for the bereaved developed by the bereaved. "At GROWW, you will find your partners in pain sharing their experience and strength. We have message boards, resource listings and secure chat rooms hosted by the most loving people on the Internet for all who are

grieving." This site has a comprehensive chat schedule and great resources. You can visit it at: http://www.groww.com or write to: 11877 Douglas Rd #102-PMB101, Alpharetta, GA 30005.

Healing Hearts
Healing Hearts leads retreats, workshops and support groups that encourage individuals to explore their personal histories and gain insights and inner peace through the healing process. You may contact them at (520) 219-8200. The mailing address is: Healing Hearts, 19627 SE 284th SE, Kent, WA 98042. You may e-mail them at grief@healinghearts.net or access their web site at: http://www.healingheart.net/.

National Self-Help Clearinghouse
The National Self-Help Clearinghouse was founded in 1976 to facilitate access to self-help groups and to increase the awareness of the importance of mutual support. The Clearinghouse conducts training activities for group leaders, carries out research activities, maintains a databank to provide information about and referrals to self-help groups, addresses professional and public policy audiences about self-help group activities, and publishes manuals, training materials and a newsletter. They offer many helpful brochures, and you can obtain more information by writing to the National Self-Help Clearinghouse at: 365 5th Avenue, Suite 3300,

New York, NY 10016 or visit their website at http://www.selfhelpweb.org/.

National Organization for Victim Assistance

This organization promotes advocacy for victim's rights, offers help for crime victims and more. They also provide a 24 hour telephone crises service for victims. The hotline number is (202) 232-6682. To learn more about their resources, visit their web site at http://www.try-nova.org or write to 1730 Park Road NW, Washington D.C. 20010 or call (202) 232-6682.

alt.support.grief Newsgroup (Internet Resource)

Newsgroup allows users to post messages on the Internet and receive responses or respond to others. The alt.support.grief offers this to its users. With Newsgroup, however, it's always good to just watch and listen and get a tone for the group before jumping in with posts. Join the newsgroup through this link: http://www.premier.net/~zoom/asg.html.

Remove Intoxicated Drivers (RID)

This national organization has 152 chapters in 41 states. Founded in 1978, this project is organized to advocate against drunk driving, educate the public and aid victims of drunk driving. You may contact RID at P.O. Box 520, Schenectady, NY 12301, call (518) 393-help or visit the website at http://www.rid-usa.org/

Sena Webzine (Internet Resource)
Sena Webzine is dedicated to the enrichment of life through developing community awareness of grief and loss issues and promoting the recognition, understanding and support of those experiencing grief and loss. The magazine is a vehicle for the safe sharing of difficult and sometimes painful experiences in all stages of life. Overcoming fear through human compassion and caring involvement is the publication's objective. You can learn more about how to receive the webzine by accessing it online at http://www.sena.org/v1i3masthead.html

The Growth House (Internet Resource)
Although this group's mission deals mostly with improving end of life care, their website has many resources that are valuable to anyone who is grieving. They also have specific pages on suicide. In addition, they offer a chat room. You can visit The Growth House at http://www.growthhouse.org

Tom Golden's Grief and Healing
Discussions Page (Internet Resource)
This site uses a web message board where you can post and respond to issues of grief and loss. Access the message board directly through the following link at: http://www.webhealing.com/cgi-bin/main.pl?.

Tragedy Assistance Program
for Survivors, Inc. (TAPS)
This is a national organization serving the families and friends of those who have died while on active military duty. You may contact them at 2001 S

Street, NW, Suite 300, Washington D.C. 20009, by calling (800) 959-TAPS, or by visiting www.taps.org.

Transformations (Internet Resource)

This well-designed site offers support in many areas, including grief. They offer a chat area and a schedule of events as well as a place to share your thoughts, stories, poetry and more. You can access the site at http://www.transformations.com/contents.html

American Suicide Foundation

This national organization offers state-by-state directories of survivor support groups for families and friends of suicide. Contact them by e-mail at 76433.1676@compuserve.com or call (800) ASF-4042. Write to: 1045 Park Avenue, New York, NY 10028.

Friends for Survival, Inc.

Organized by and for survivors, this non-profit group offers its services at no cost to those who have lost a loved one to suicide. Resources include a newsletter, referalls to local support groups, a list of suggested resources and more. You may contact them at Friends for Survival, Inc., Post Office Box 214463, Sacramento, California 95821. Call (916) 392-0664. They also have a Suicide Loss Helpline—(800) 646-7322.

General books for adults

A Time to Grieve: Meditations for Healing After the Death of a Loved One by Carol Staudacher,

Harpercollins, 1994—365 daily readings offer comfort, insight and hope. This book is written specifically for people after the death of a loved one, however it is appropriate for anyone who still copes with the effects of a loss of any kind. A great gift for yourself or a grieving friend.

Beyond Grief by Carol Staudacher, New Harbinger Publications, 1987—This book is about understanding and then coping with loss, with clearly stated suggestions for each part of the grieving process. Written both for the bereaved and the helping professional, it combines supportive personal stories with a step-by-step approach to recovery. *Beyond Grief* acknowledges the path, reassures and counsels. Includes guidelines to create support groups and guidelines for helping others. It says to the grieving person: you are not alone, you can get through the pain, and there is a path back to feeling alive again.

Companion Through Darkness: Inner Dialogues on Grief by Stephanie Ericsson, Harperperennial Library, 1993—As a result of her own experience with many kinds of loss, the author offers an intimate, touching guide for those in grief. The book combines excerpts from her own diary writings with brief essays.

Complicated Losses, Difficult Deaths: A Practical Guide for Working Through Grief by Roslyn A. Karaban, Ph.D., Resource Publications, 1999— Written by a pastoral counselor, certified grief therapist and death educator, the book deals with losses that are more difficult to cope with than others: suicide, sudden loss, the death of a child and murders among otherslosses—that evoke grief reactions and symptoms that are more intense and last longer than "ordinary" grief.

Dreams that Help You Mourn by Lois Lindsey Hendricks. Resource Publications, 1997—This book will put you in the company of other mourners and their dreams. You'll learn that dreaming after losing a loved one is absolutely normal. In fact, it's the soul's way of mourning. The book will help you take better advantage of the healing power of your dreams.

I Can't Get Over It: A Handbook for Trauma Survivors by Aphrodite Matsakis, New Harbinger Publications, Inc., 1996—Explains how post-traumatic stress disorder (PTSD) affects survivors of a variety of traumas including disasters, rape, crime and violence. Addresses the survivor directly and helps them self-diagnose to then get appropriate treatment. Includes a variety of techniques and self-help suggestions for safe recovery.

In Memoriam: A Practical Guide to Planning a Memorial Service by Amanda Bennett and Terence B. Foley, Simon and Schuster Adult Publishing Group, 1997—Written in an easy-to-read format, this book provides a full range of options to help you choose music, arrange flowers, select a format, prepare a eulogy and invite speakers and offers a wide range of selected appropriate readings.

Life After Loss: A Personal Guide Dealing with Death, Divorce, Job Change and Relocation by Bob Deits, Da Capo Press, 2004. Provides skills for healthy recovery, including how to cry, how to write a goodbye letter, how to deal with emotions and how to cope.

Moving Beyond Grief: Lessons from Those who Have Lived through Sorrow by Ruth Sissom, Discovery House, 1994—A religiously oriented book offering stories of persons who have learned to cope with grief and trauma.

The Courage to Grieve by Judy Tatelbaum, HarperCollins Publishers, 1984—This book covers many aspects of grief and resolution. Divided into five sections, it explores the grief experience and creative recovery.

What to Do When a Loved One Dies: A Practical and Compassionate Guide to Dealing with Death on Life's Terms, by Eva Shaw, Dickens Press, 1994— Presents excellent guidelines describing what to do when a death occurs. It has an extensive listing of support groups, resources and other sources of help. The approach is extremely detailed and includes sections on dealing with catastrophic deaths.

Books about grief recovery

Grief's Courageous Journey: A Workbook by Sandi Caplan and Gordon Lang, New Harbinger Publications, 1995—Grieving the loss of a loved one is an intensely personal process. This workbook takes the hand of those who are left behind and guides them, at their own pace, along the path of their own healing journey. It provides a compassionate program for coping with day-to-day life and accepting the changes in yourself and others. Guided by a sequence of journaling exercises and suggestions for creating healing personal rituals, you can use the workbook to tell the story of your relationship with the person who died, grieve your loss and safely remember the past. You will also learn techniques for redefining your present life and re-creating your sense of future. The book includes a comprehensive ten-session facilitator's guide for creating a grief support group in your community.

Healing our Losses: A Journal for Working Through Your Grief by Jack Miller, Ph.D., Resource Publications, 1994—The author shares experiences of loss in his own life and will guide you to record your memories, thoughts, and feelings about loss in your life. Journaling may be done alone or in a group setting.

Healing the Heart; Letting Go; Therapeutic Stories for Trauma and Stress; Stories to Heal the Grieving Heart (AUDIO TAPES), N. Davis, 1995, 6178 Oxon Hill Rd., Suite 306, Oxon Hill, MD, (301) 567-9297—These audio tapes contain collections of therapeutic stories designed to ease the process of grieving, explain stages of grief, address the intuitive side of the mind and help the listener find what he/she needs within the self. Visual imagery and relaxation exercises are also included.

Managing Traumatic Stress through Art: Drawing from the Center by Barry M. Cohen, Mary-Michola Barnes and Anita B. Rankin, Sidran Institute Press. 1996—Provides step-by-step art experiences designed to help the reader understand, manage and transform the after effects of trauma. Written in a practical, useful style that shows the ways in which art making and writing can assist one's healing from severe trauma.

Books for grieving men

Griefquest : Men Coping With Loss by Robert Miller, St. Mary's Press, 1999—*GriefQuest* is a book of meditations written for men and the women who love and care about them. This book, written by other men, helps make sense out of the unique challenges that grief and loss force on men today.

Grief Therapy for Men by Linus Mundy, Abbey Press, 1998—This little book acknowledges the uniqueness of male grief and offers men real permission to grieve. It gives a host of practical suggestions for healthy male grief—what to do, what not to do, when to act boldly and when to just "be."

Men & Grief: A Guide for Men Surviving the Death of a Loved One by Carol Staudacher, New Harbinger Publications, 1991—*Men & Grief* is the first book to look in depth at the unique patterns of male bereavement. Based on extensive interviews with male survivors, it describes the four characteristics of male grief, explains the forces that shape and influence male grief and provides step-by-step help for the male survivor.

When Men Grieve : Why Men Grieve Differently and How You Can Help by Elizabeth Levang, Fairview, 1998— Insightful text on the unique characteristics of men's grief and how they face loss. Includes poetry and strategies for partners, friends and relatives.

Books about the loss of a friend

Grieving the Death of a Friend by Harold Ivan Smith, Augsburg Fortress Publications, 1996—The death of a friend is one of the most significant but unrecognized experiences of grief in American culture. This unique new book moves with, rather than against, the natural grief process by exploring its many aspects—the friending, the passing, the burying, the mourning, the remembering and the reconciling.

When a Friend Dies: A Book for Teens about Grieving and Healing by Marilyn E. Gootman, Ed.D., 1994, Free Spirit Publishing, Minneapolis, MN—A small, powerful book whose author has seen her own children suffer from the death of a friend. She knows first hand what teenagers go through when another teen dies. Very easy to read, some of the questions dealt with include: How long will this last? Is it wrong to go to parties and have fun? How can I find a counselor or therapist? What is normal?

Books about helping someone who is grieving

The Art of Condolence by Leonard M Zunin, M.D & Hilary Stanton Zunin, HarperCollins, 1992—Offers specific and wise advice for responding to another's grief. Discusses what to write, what to say and what to do.

When Your Friend's Child Dies: A Guide to Being a Thoughtful and Caring Friend by Julane Grant, Angel Hugs Publishing, 1998—A simply written, straight-forward book that will tell you what to say and do when you have a friend whose child has died. And, just as important, Chapter One tells you what not to say and why. An early reader described this book as a "slap-in-the-face wake-up call." After reading this book, you will know how to comfort a parent who has lost a child, even ten years later.

You Can Help Someone Who's Grieving : A How-To Healing Handbook by Victoria Frigo, iUniverse, 2000—A practical resource that deals with such issues as what to say and not to say after someone dies, how long the grieving period lasts and its many stages, how to write sympathy notes and how to handle holidays and anniversaries.

Books about losing a parent

How to Survive the Loss of a Parent: A Guide for Adults by Lois F. Akner, Catherine Whitney, HarperCollins, 1994—Therapist and author, Lois Akner, explains why the loss of a parent is different from other losses and using examples from her experience, shows how it is possible to work through the grief.

Losing a Parent: Passage to a New Way of Living by Alexandra Kennedy, Harper San Francisco, 1991—Based on the author's personal experience, she writes on topics such as keeping a journal, saying goodbye, tending to your wounds and the "living parent within you."

Losing a Parent: A Personal Guide to Coping with that Special Grief that Comes with Losing a Parent by Fiona Marshall, 1993, Fisher Books—Offers comforting and inspiring advice for helping one cope with the different and difficult effects of loss. The author includes insightful and practical strategies to use in dealing with the surviving parent and other family members. Looks at the impact of the sudden death of a parent as well as terminal illness. It also includes suggestions on how to locate help and inheritance issues.

Mid-Life Orphan: Facing Life's Changes Now that Your Parents are Gone by Jane Brooks, Berkley books, 1999—Many mid-life orphans feel isolated, even abandoned, when their parents die, but they also learn how to cope and extract life lessons from their experience. This book focuses on a loss that has been a fact of life for centuries, but has moved to the forefront as baby boomers, who represent 1/3 of the U.S. population, are forced to deal with this age of loss.

Motherless Daughters: The Legacy of Loss by Hope Edelman, Dell Publishing Company, 1995—Includes stories of women whose mothers have died early in their lives and how the absence of a mother shapes one's identity.

The Loss That is Forever: The Lifelong Impact of the Early Death of a Mother or Father by Maxine Harris, Ph.D., Plume, 1996—Explores the impact that early loss of a parent has on every aspect of development. Who one becomes, how one loves, how one parents, and what one believes about the world are all shaped by the experience of this loss. Provides comfort and guidance for coping and shows how the human spirit can survive and master this loss.

"What the caterpillar calls
the end of the world, the
master calls a butterfly."
~ **Richard Bach**

Online Support Classes, Groups and Resources

Take a step toward healing with interactive, online courses led by best-selling author Brook Noel

How do the classes work?

Its easy to get started with a GriefSteps class. Simply enroll in the class of your choice at www.griefsteps.com We offer a wide variety of classes ranging in price from $19 to $129.

What do I get with my class?

1. Once you enroll, you'll receive a welcome packet that will contain directions for the classes.

2. Each class has "assignments" that you can turn in for comments from Brook Noel.

3. Each class also has a message board where you can post questions and talk to other students.

4. There is also a designated weekly, one-hour "chat" time for each class. You can log on to the private chat to talk about your experiences and assignments. These chats are moderated by Brook Noel.

*Participate in chats, message boards and assignments is optional.

Healing Exercises – Part One

In this interactive, online course, you'll complete 10 different exercises that help you move forward through grief and resolve open issues. The exercises can be completed again and again after the class to further

your healing. Brook Noel will comment on work you choose to turn in and encourage you in your journey.
Class length – 6 weeks   Cost $49

Now What? Living After Loss

This class offers a solid foundation for anyone wondering how to go on after loss. You'll learn what to expect physically and emotionally and how to take your first steps toward healing.
Class length – 3 weeks   Cost $19

Rituals to Honor Your Loved One

Rituals are a wonderful way to keep the memory of your loved one with you. This class will introduce you to different types of rituals and guide you in creating one of your own.
Class length – 4 weeks   Cost $29

When Will the Pain End?
Working through Unresolved Grief

Throughout this 10 week course, you'll learn about the different stages of grief and how to recognize which of your life losses have not been grieved completely. You'll learn exercises and tactics to heal and work through unresolved grief, which are the most common causes of sadness and depression. This is the perfect class for anyone who is having difficulty moving forward after a life loss.
Class length – 10 weeks   Cost $99

The Healing Journey: Writing through Grief

In this writing-intensive class, you'll learn how to write the story of your loss and discover its meaning. You'll create a record of your cherished memories and discover how your loved one is still in your life today. When you complete this class you'll have a very special chronicle of you and your loved ones relationship.
Class length – 12 weeks   Cost $129

How to Create Your Own Support Group

In this class you will be given assignments that will lead to the creation of your own support group by the completion of the course. You'll decide what type of support group you want to start (online or in-person), create materials to help spread the word and learn how to successfully guide your support group meetings.

Class length – 8 weeks   Cost $79

Basic Strategies and Exercises for Healing

In this interactive, online course, you'll complete 4 different exercises that can help you on your grief journey. You'll also learn what to expect on your journey and strategies for coping.

Class length – 3 weeks   Cost $19

Take a step toward healing.
Enroll today at www.griefsteps.com

Grief Resources from Grief Steps®

I Wasn't Ready to Say Goodbye: Surviving, Coping and Healing After the Sudden Death of a Loved One by Pamela D. Blair, Ph.D. and Brook Noel (14.95) ISBN 1-891400-27-4; Companion Workbook also available (18.95) ISBN 1-891400-50-9

Grief Steps: 10 Steps to Regroup, Rebuild and Renew After Any Life Loss by Brook Noel ($14.95) ISBN 1-891400-35-5; Companion Workbook also available ($18.95) ISBN 1-891400-34-7

Living with Grief: a guide for year first year of grieving by Pamela D. Blair, Ph.D. and Brook Noel ($8.95) adapted from *I Wasn't Ready to Say Goodbye: Surviving, Coping and Healing After the Sudden Death of a Loved One* ISBN 1-891400-08-8

Surviving Holidays, Birthdays and Anniversaries: A Guide for Grieving During Special Occasions by Brook Noel ($8.95) ISBN 1-891400-03-7

You're Not Alone: Resources to Help You On Your Grief Journey by Brook Noel and Pamela D. Blair, Ph.D. ($9.95) ISBN 1-891400-63-0

Understanding the Emotional and Physical Effects of Grief by Brook Noel ($9.95) ISBN 1-891400-77-0

Finding Peace: Exercises to Help Heal the Pain of Loss by Brook Noel and Pamela D. Blair, Ph.D. ($9.95) ISBN 1-891400-78-9

My World is Upside Down: Making Sense of Life After Confronting Death by Brook Noel and Pamela D. Blair, Ph.D. ($9.95) ISBN 1-891400-24-X